Beautiful Bows

Beautiful Bows

Inspirational Ideas for Decorating Flowers, Crafts and Gifts

APPLE

A Creative Publishing international book

First published in the UK
by Apple Press in 2005
4th Floor
Sheridan House
112-116a Western Road
Hove BN3 1DD
United Kingdom

www.apple-press.com

ISBN 1-84543-040-9

Intitial publication in the United States under the title *Creative Bows Made Easy*

Printed in China:
10 9 8 7 6 5 4 3 2 1

Many thanks to Berwick Offray
LLC for providing their beautiful
ribbons and creative bow designs.
You can find their ribbon, under
the brand names Offray and Lion,
at craft, fabric and other retail
stores around the world. Special
thanks to Barry Sokol, Vice
President of Craft/Floral Sales, for
his support of this project.

Contents

Creating Bows	6
Ribbons	8
Shoestring	**13**
Two Loops	**17**
Two Loops and a Center	**21**
Four Loops and a Center	**25**
Skinny Loops	**29**
Tailored	**33**
Creative Ideas	*36*
Loops in a Row	**39**
Floral Pick	**43**
One-Sided	**47**
Pompom	**51**
Starburst	**55**
Floral	**59**
Asymmetrical Layers	**63**
Grand	**67**
Bow Combinations	*70*

Curled	**73**
Wall Display	**77**
Fan	**81**
Pinwheel	**85**
Poinsettia	**89**
Gathered Rose	**93**
Luxury Rose	*96*

Creating Bows

*L*OVELY BOWS ARE EVERYWHERE! They grace gift packages, floral designs, fashion accessories, craft projects, and home décor items. Bows are colorful and textured, sentimental and festive. Some are neat and tiny while others are bountiful. Now *you* can make perfect bows for every occasion and purpose, following the step-by-step directions and illustrations in this book. There are twenty basic bows and lots of variations and combinations to choose from. Multiply that by an unlimited selection of ribbons, and you have the formula for making hundreds of unique, creative bows.

How much ribbon? The amount of ribbon needed to make a bow depends on how large you want it to be and what width of ribbon you use. The amounts and types of ribbon needed to make the bows in the photographs are given in the materials lists. If you want your bows to be larger or smaller, increase or decrease the amounts. It is often a good idea to draw the ribbon from the reel as you form the bow, and cut it only after you are satisfied with the bow size.

Materials. Bow-making doesn't require any special equipment or craft materials. A ruler, scissors, craft wire, wire cutter, and glue are all that you need for most bows.

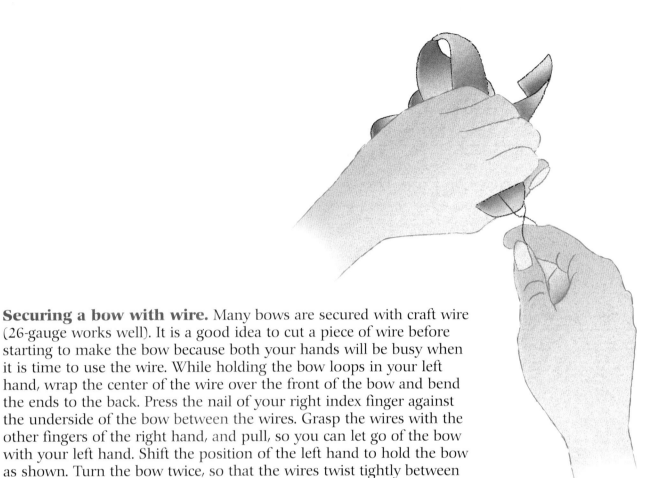

Securing a bow with wire. Many bows are secured with craft wire (26-gauge works well). It is a good idea to cut a piece of wire before starting to make the bow because both your hands will be busy when it is time to use the wire. While holding the bow loops in your left hand, wrap the center of the wire over the front of the bow and bend the ends to the back. Press the nail of your right index finger against the underside of the bow between the wires. Grasp the wires with the other fingers of the right hand, and pull, so you can let go of the bow with your left hand. Shift the position of the left hand to hold the bow as shown. Turn the bow twice, so that the wires twist tightly between your right index finger and the bow back. In the illustration, the wires have been twisted once.

Tips. Here are a few hints to get you started and help you make great looking bows every time.

- If you are a beginner, start with some simple bows from the beginning of the book. In no time, you'll be able to make anything in the book.

- Practice the "wire twist" a couple of times. A tight twist is essential for a secure, professional-looking bow.

- Ribbons with wired edges can be easier to work with. You can position them as you like, and they'll stay put.

- Double-face ribbon (the same on both sides) makes some bows a bit easier.

- After you make a bow, take a few seconds to arrange and fluff the loops. Then hold up the bow and admire what you've created!

Ribbons

Ribbons are available in an amazing range of styles, textures, and colors, with choices suitable for every occasion and purpose. They come in many widths, ranging from 1/16" to 3½" (1.5 to 89 mm) and even wider. Most fabric, or fashion, ribbons are purchased by the yard (meter). Giftwrap and craft ribbons are usually sold by the reel. Fashion ribbons are like tiny fabrics, woven to a specific width with finished edges called selvages. They may have fine wires woven into the edges, which help you shape the bows. Giftwrap and craft ribbons are generally nonwoven (more like paper) with cut, sealed edges that don't ravel. Some are cut from wide fabrics and their edges are stitched to keep them from raveling.

Which ribbons you choose for your bows depends on where they will be used, the effect you want to create, and how long you want them to last. Fabric ribbons are generally more expensive than craft and giftwrap ribbons. They produce luxurious, long-lasting bows most suitable for fashion accessories or décor accents. However, they can also be used for special gifts. Less expensive ribbons are often chosen for gifts, especially when they will likely be tossed away with the wrapping paper. Cost is also an important consideration if you need lots of bows for a special celebration.

Satins. Woven to produce a glossy, smooth surface on both sides (double-face [1]) or one side (single-face [2]), satin ribbons are suitable for many bows. They come in a rainbow of solid colors with plain or feather-edge (3) finishes. Some satin ribbons are printed with a floral design or softly blended stripes (4). Others may have sheer stripes (5) running through them.

Taffetas. Taffeta ribbons have a fine, plain weave that makes them reversible with smooth, slightly lustrous surfaces. Often they have fine copper wires woven into the selvages for extra body and to allow them to be shaped. Taffeta ribbons include ombré and variegated styles (6) that shade from dark to light or from one color to another across the ribbon width. There are also taffetas with woven plaids and checks (7). Shot-effect taffetas (8) are woven with contrasting colors in the warp and weft that create an iridescent look. Moiré taffetas (9) have a watermark design embossed onto the surface.

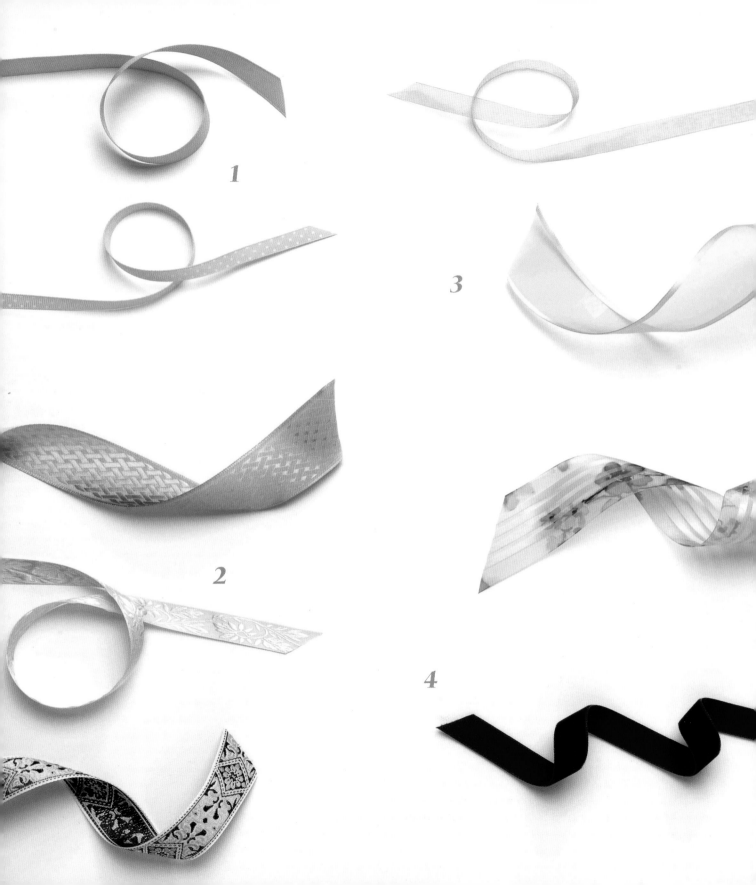

1

2

3

4

Grosgrains (1). The weave structure of grosgrain ribbons creates a matte appearance with a distinctive crosswise rib. These sturdy fabric ribbons are available in solid colors as well as striped, dotted, and patterned styles.

Jacquards (2). These ribbons feature woven-in designs, either single color or multicolor, that resemble miniature tapestries. Metallic threads may be incorporated into the designs, which include florals, geometrics, and other figures. Jacquard ribbons are single-face, making them most suitable for bows where only one side of the ribbon is visible, such as a tailored bow, a fan bow, or a pinwheel.

Sheers (3). Finely woven, transparent ribbons in a range of widths are used to create gossamer, feminine effects. Many have monofilament woven into the selvages for support; wired-edge sheer ribbons are also available. Sheer ribbons often have satin or metallic stripes.

Velvets (4). Like velvet fabric, these ribbons have a cut pile that is soft and luxurious to the touch and gives extra depth to their colors.

Craft and giftwrap ribbons. Available in woven and nonwoven styles, they are generally stiffer than fashion ribbons, either because of their fiber content or the way they are manufactured. Some craft ribbons are stiffened fabric with merrowed edges (**5**), meaning wire is caught under serged stitches along both sides. Florist ribbon (**6**) is shiny on one side and matte on the other with cut, rather than woven, edges. Curling ribbon (**7**) is available in lots of solid colors as well as prints, metallics, and holographic styles. It is specially designed to coil into tight ringlets when it is drawn across a hard edge, such as the dull side of a scissors blade.

Shoestring

*T*HIS BOW IS MADE THE WAY SOME PEOPLE TIE THEIR SHOELACES, by making two loops and tying them together. Shoestring bows of narrow ribbons are useful for decorating stationery or as pretty accents on memory album pages. Because they can be tied quickly, shoestring bows are also a good choice when you need to make lots of bows for party favors or Christmas cards. When made from wider satin or grosgrain ribbon, this simple bow can be worn in the hair or tied around the handles of a gift bag or basket.

You will need

18" (46 cm) ribbon, ⅝" (15 mm) wide

Scissors

Shoestring

1. Form two equal loops in the ribbon, one on each side of the center. Hold one in each hand, with the loops upward and the tails down.

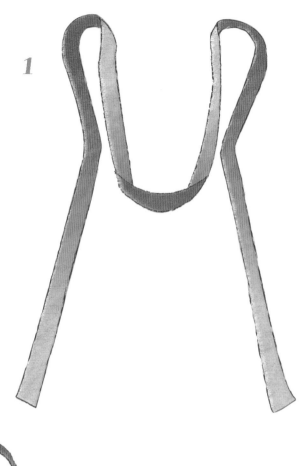

1

2

2. Cross the right loop over the left loop, creating a circle in the ribbon below the loops.

3

3. Wrap the right loop behind the left loop, through the lower circle, and back to the front. Allow the tail of the right side to flip over the bow center.

4. Pull the loops in opposite directions to form the bow. Pull on the tails to adjust the bow until the loops are even, the tails are equal in length, and the center wrap is neat.

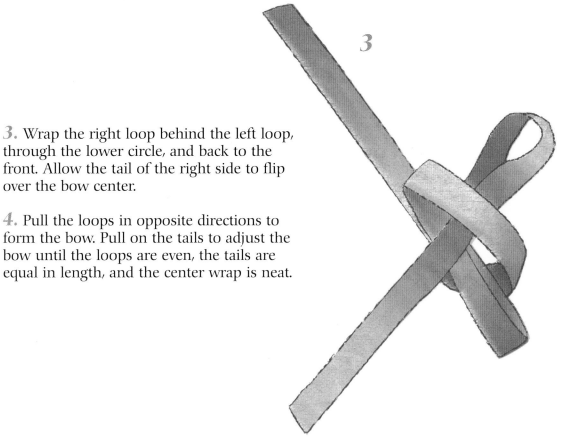

Two Loops

THIS IS A VERY SIMPLE BOW TO MAKE and can be done with almost any type and width of ribbon. Two-loop bows make beautiful hair accessories, wedding accents, or Christmas tree decorations. When making bows for tree decorations or gift wrap, leave the wire tails long for attaching the bow. Rather than wrapping the center with ribbon, you can add a ribbon rose or silk flower to the center of the bow to hide the wire. For a different finish, tie a knot at the end of each tail.

You will need

28" (71 cm) ribbon, ⅛", ³⁄₁₆", ¼", ⅜", ½", or ⅝" (3, 5, 7, 9, 12, or 15 mm) wide

or 32" (81.5 cm) ribbon, 1½" (39 mm) wide or wider

or 22" (56 cm) cording

Scissors

26-gauge craft wire

Wire cutter

Glue

Two Loops

1. Cut a 9" (23 cm) length of wire, and set it aside. Cut a 4" (10 cm) piece of ribbon for the center wrap, and set it aside.

2. Lay the remaining ribbon face down on the work surface and fold the ends in, crossing them at the center of the ribbon. Adjust the loops to the desired size.

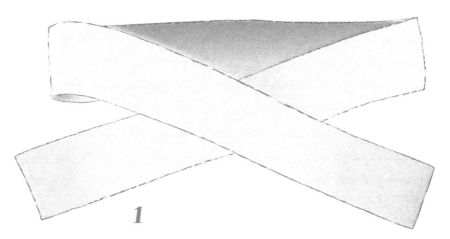

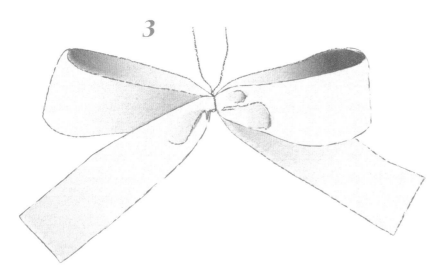

3. Gather all three layers together at the center and pinch tightly between the thumb and index finger of your left hand. Pick up the bow, and use the right hand to wrap the center with wire (page 7). Leave the wire tails long for attaching the bow, and spread them apart to the sides. Or trim the wire short.

4. Wrap the reserved piece of ribbon around the bow center, covering the wire. Overlap the ends at the bow back. Turn under the overlapping end and glue in place.

5. Trim the bow tails diagonally or in an inverted V.

4

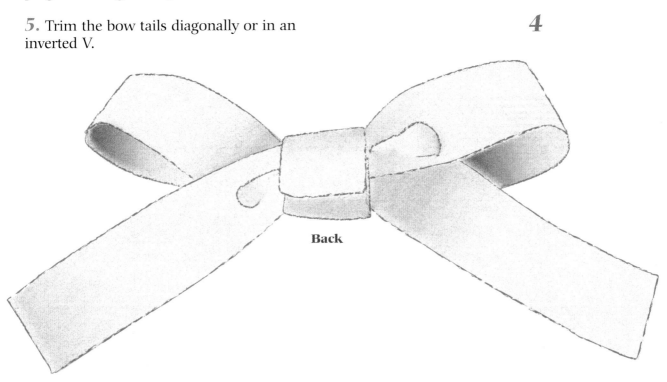

Back

Two Loops
And a Center

THIS BOW HAS A CENTER LOOP, or nose, that adds interest and hides the wire. The two-loop bow with a center is often made with ribbon 2¼" to 3" (56 to 77 mm) wide. When made from elegant ribbon, like the floral printed satin with sheer edges, shown at left, the bow can be used for a romantic fashion accent. The tails can be cut short or left long to catch the breeze. The same bow made from craft ribbon can dress up a floral arrangement or adorn a gift bag.

You will need

*1 to 1½ yd. (0.92 to 1.4 m) ribbon,
 2¼" to 3" (56 to 77 mm) wide*

Scissors

26-gauge craft wire

Wire cutter

Two Loops and a Center

1. Cut a 9" (23 cm) length of wire, and set it aside. Pick up the ribbon in your left hand, about 8" (20.5 cm) from the end, with the right side facing you. Gather the ribbon and pinch it tightly between the thumb and index finger, with the fingers pointing up, leaving the tail hanging to the right and the working end of the ribbon to the left.

2. With the working end of the ribbon, form a loop of the desired size. Gather the ribbon at the base of the loop, slip it under the first layer, and hold the layers together. Now you have a tail on the right and one loop on the left.

2

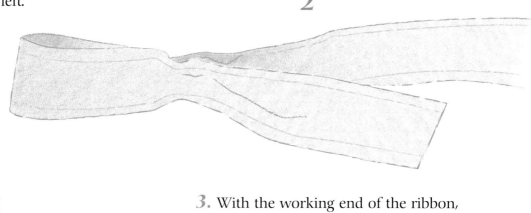

3

3. With the working end of the ribbon, form a loop of the same size on the right. Pinch the ribbon together at the base of the second loop, slip it under your thumb over the other layers and hold the layers together.

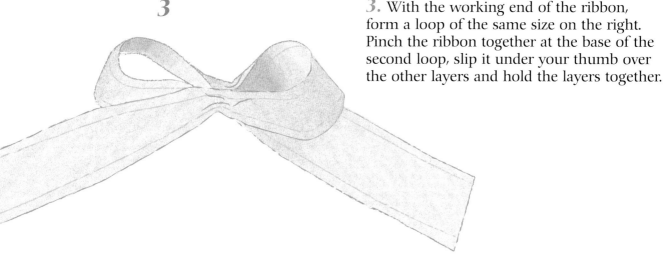

4

4. If the ribbon is double-face, wrap the working end around your thumb and through the hole between your thumb and index finger, forming a small center loop. Slip the base of the center loop under your thumb over the other layers, and hold the layers together. If the ribbon is single-face, twist it once before forming the center loop, so the right side faces out.

5. Insert the wire through the center loop from top to bottom. Slip the wire under your thumb, between the ribbon tails. Wrap the bow center with wire (page 7). Leave the wire ends long for attaching the bow, or cut them short.

6. Trim the bow tails diagonally to the desired length. Adjust the loops and tails.

Four Loops
And a Center

SIMILAR TO THE TWO-LOOP BOW WITH A CENTER, this bow simply has another loop on each side. It has enough presence to be used alone to embellish a gift that is too difficult to wrap. Made from 7/8" (23 mm) velvet or double-face satin ribbon, this bow would make a lovely hair adornment for a young girl on a special occasion. In wired-edge metallic ribbon, the four-loop bow with a center would be a festive addition to a holiday wreath. The size of the loops should be in scale to the ribbon width. The bow at left was made from 1½" (39 mm) wired-edge satin ribbon and the loops are 3½" (9 cm) long.

You will need

1 to 2 yd. (0.92 to 1.85 m) ribbon,
  7/8" to 3" (23 to 77 mm) wide

Scissors

26-gauge craft wire

Wire cutter

Four Loops and a Center

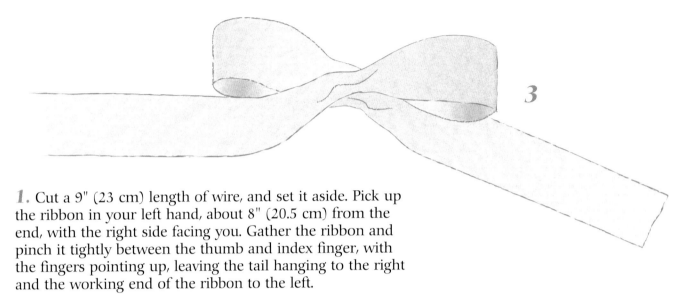

3

1. Cut a 9" (23 cm) length of wire, and set it aside. Pick up the ribbon in your left hand, about 8" (20.5 cm) from the end, with the right side facing you. Gather the ribbon and pinch it tightly between the thumb and index finger, with the fingers pointing up, leaving the tail hanging to the right and the working end of the ribbon to the left.

2. With the working end of the ribbon, form a loop of the desired size. Gather the ribbon at the base of the loop, slip it under the first layer, and hold the layers together. Now you have a tail on the right and one loop on the left.

3. With the working end of the ribbon, form a loop of the same size on the right. Pinch the ribbon together at the base of the second loop, slip it under your thumb over the other layers and hold the layers together.

4

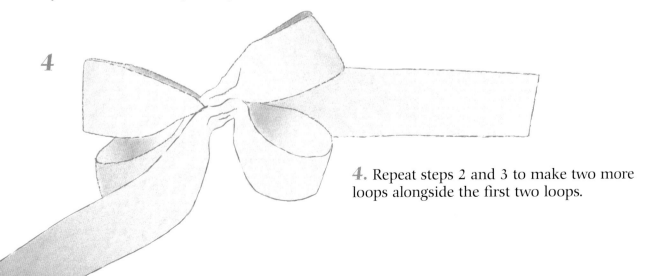

4. Repeat steps 2 and 3 to make two more loops alongside the first two loops.

5

5. If the ribbon is double-face, wrap the working end around your thumb and through the hole between your thumb and index finger, forming a small center loop. Slip the base of the center loop under your thumb over the other layers, and hold the layers together. If the ribbon is single-face, twist it once before forming the center loop, so the right side faces out.

6. Insert the wire through the center loop from top to bottom. Slip the wire under your thumb, between the ribbon tails. Wrap the bow center with wire (page 7). Leave the wire ends long for attaching the bow, or cut them short.

7. Trim the bow tails diagonally to the desired length. Adjust the loops and tails.

Skinny Loops

A BOW WITH OODLES OF SKINNY LOOPS is a cute addition to a decorative accessory in a nursery. A skinny-loop bow could also embellish a small gift or an ornament. This type of bow is made from ribbon ¹⁄₁₆" to ³⁄₈" (1.5 to 9 mm) wide. Double-face ribbon is recommended because both sides will be seen. This same technique can be used to make raffia bows for trimming a country-styled Christmas tree or evergreen swag. Narrow decorative cording and bright tubular ribbons can be tied in skinny loops bows for a playful giftwrap finish.

*Y*ou will need

2 to 3 yd. (1.85 to 2.75 m)
  narrow ribbon or raffia

Scissors

Skinny Loops

1. Pick up the ribbon in your left hand with the right side facing you. Hold the ribbon between the thumb and index finger, with the fingers pointing up, leaving a tail of the desired length hanging to the right and the working end of the ribbon to the left.

2. With the working end of the ribbon, form a loop of the desired size. At the base of the loop, slip it under the first layer, and hold the layers together. Now you have a tail on the right and one loop on the left.

3. With the working end of the ribbon, form a loop of the same size on the right. At the base of the second loop, slip it under your thumb over the other layers and hold the layers together.

4. Repeat steps 2 and 3 until you have made the desired number of loops, keeping the loops about the same size with the same number of loops to the right and left. Cut off the left ribbon tail at the same length as the right one.

5. Wrap the remaining ribbon around the center of the loops; hold it in place between your finger and thumb. Tie it tightly in back. (This can be a little awkward; a second pair of hands is helpful.) Trim the ends to the desired length, leaving two more tails.

5

Tailored

THE TAILORED BOW, ALSO CALLED A DIOR BOW,
is made of nearly flat, stacked loops that graduate in size. When
made from wide satin ribbon, a tailored bow can become a hair
accessory, a hat embellishment, or an accent on a formal dress.
It can be used for gift-wrapping or as an embellishment on a
wedding guest book, as shown at left. Because it is important to
always keep the right side of the ribbon facing out, there are different sets of instructions for double-face and single-face ribbon.

You will need

45" (115 cm) ribbon, 1½" (39 mm) wide

Scissors

Stapler

Glue

Tailored: Double-Face Ribbon

1. Hold the ribbon end between your left thumb and index finger, with the fingers pointing up and the working end of the ribbon to the left. Turn under the working end of the ribbon, forming a loop to the left of your thumb. Hold the layers together flat between your thumb and finger. The working end of the ribbon is now on the right.

2. Turn under the working end of the ribbon, forming a loop of the same size to the right of your thumb. Hold the layers together flat between your thumb and finger. The working end of the ribbon is now on the left.

3. Form two more layers of loops, increasing the loop size with each layer and keeping the ribbon flat between your thumb and finger. Staple all the layers together at the center. Trim away the excess ribbon on the bow back.

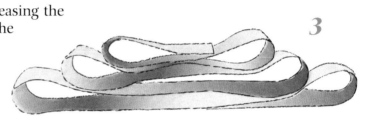

4. From the remaining ribbon, cut a length of ribbon 2" to 3" (5 to 7.5 cm) longer than the bottom layer of loops. Cut an inverted V in each end, and staple it beneath the loop layers.

5. Cut a length of ribbon three times the ribbon width. Wrap it around the center of the bow, keeping the layers flat. Overlap the ends at the bow back. Turn under the overlapping end and glue in place.

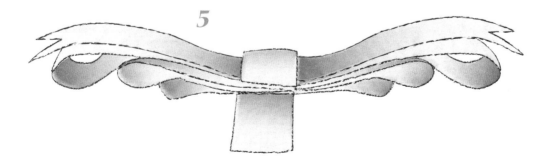

Tailored: Single–Face Ribbon

1. Cut the ribbon in three different lengths, each slightly longer than twice the desired length of the loop layer.

2. For each layer, fold the ends under to the center and staple in place.

3. Place the loop layers on top of one another in graduated sizes and staple them together.

4. Follow steps 4 and 5 opposite to complete the bow.

2

Creative Ideas

Pin a jeweled brooch to the center of a tailored bow (page 33) to make a glamorous fashion accessory. Secure the bow to an evening handbag or hat, or wear it at your waist.

Add interest to the center wrap of a two-loop bow (page 18) by tying a loose overhand knot in the ribbon strip before wrapping it around the middle of the bow.

Streamers for a flower girl's hair wreath can be made by following the directions for the skinny loops bow (page 30). Using multiple ribbons, make the loops and tails extra-long and tie tiny knots in the tails at various places to add texture.

Turn a four-loop bow (page 25) into a butterfly. Form four loops without tails from 1½" (39 mm) ribbon, making the upper loops slightly larger. Wire them together with tails made from narrower, wired-edge ribbon. String three beads onto decorative wire. Wrap the decorative wire around the center of the bow and shape the ends into antennas.

37

Loops in a Row

THIS IS AN IDEAL GIFT PACKAGE BOW and can be made in any ribbon width, scaled to the size of the package. For best results, use double-face ribbon. To make the bow with single-face ribbon, follow the same instructions, but twist the ribbon after forming each loop to keep the right side facing out. Secure the ribbon to the package parallel to the wrapping ribbons, either across the center of the package or diagonally across one corner.

You will need

1½ yd. (1.4 m) ribbon in the desired width

Scissors

26-gauge craft wire

Wire cutter

Loops in a Row

1. Cut a 9" (23 cm) length of wire, and set it aside. Form a small loop at one end of the ribbon. Slip your thumb into the loop and pinch the base of the loop tightly between the thumb and index finger, with the fingers pointing up, and the working end of the ribbon to the right.

2. Turn under the working end of the ribbon, forming a slightly larger loop to the right of the center loop. Pinch it together at the base and hold it beneath the first two layers. The working end of the ribbon is now on the left.

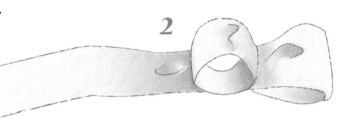

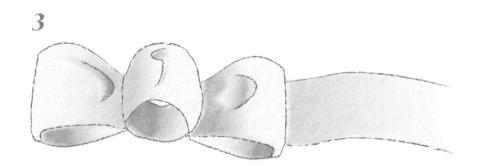

3. Turn under the working end of the ribbon, forming a loop to the left of the center loop, the same size as the second loop. Pinch it together at the base and hold it beneath the other layers. The working end of the ribbon is now on the right.

4. Repeat steps 2 and 3 twice, making each layer of loops slightly larger than the previous one.

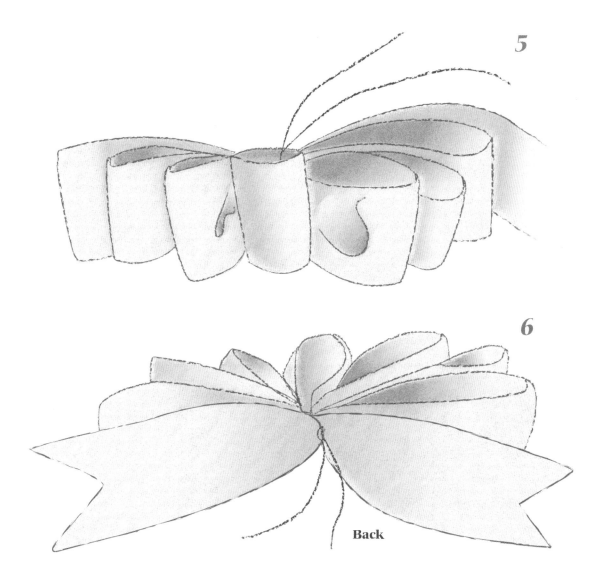

5 **6**

Back

5. Insert the wire through the center loop from top to bottom. Slip the wire under your thumb. Wrap the bow center with wire (page 7). Leave the wire ends long.

6. Cut off the remaining ribbon; center it on the back of the bow, parallel to the loops. Wire it in place, forming two tails. Trim the bow tails in an inverted V at the desired length.

Floral Pick

THIS SIMPLE BOW IS ATTACHED TO A WOODEN PICK for inserting into a potted plant or a fresh, dried, or silk flower arrangement. The tails, about the same length as the loops, are turned upward in the same direction as the loops. Several floral pick bows inserted throughout a bridal bouquet or low, round floral arrangement add color and a pleasing texture. If the floral pick bows are used in fresh floral arrangements or plants, the picks should be wrapped with floral tape to prevent water from wicking up onto the ribbon.

You will need

*1¼ yd. (1.15 m) ribbon,
 1½" (39 mm) wide*

Scissors

Wooden floral pick with wire

Floral tape, optional

Floral Pick

1. Pinch the ribbon together tightly between the thumb and index finger 3" (7.5 cm) from the end, with the short tail pointing upward.

2. Turn the working end of the ribbon upward, just below your fingers. Pinch the ribbon and hold it together with the first layer.

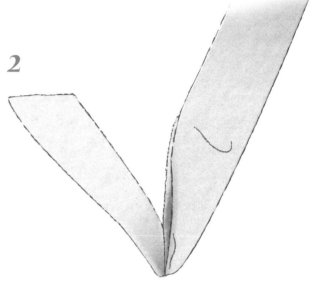

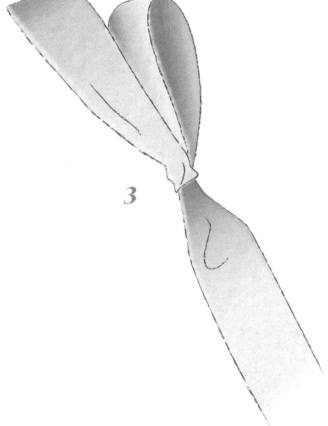

3. Form a loop. Pinch the ribbon at the base of the loop and hold it together with the other layers.

4. Repeat steps 2 and 3 until you have three or four loops.

5. Repeat step 2 and cut the ribbon, leaving a tail the same length as the first tail.

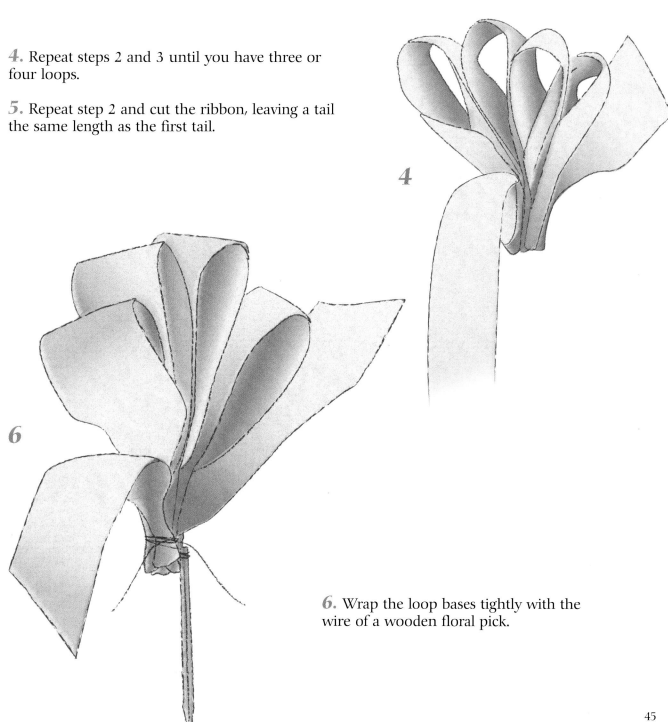

4

6

6. Wrap the loop bases tightly with the wire of a wooden floral pick.

One-Sided

*T*HIS BOW IS IDEAL FOR A BASKET HANDLE or the front of a gift bag. Three coordinating ribbons form multiple upward loops with a lavish cascade of six flowing tails. If desired, the bow could also be made using only one ribbon. In these instructions, each layer is formed and wired separately and then the layers are joined together. As you become more adept at making the bow, you can form and hold all the layers at once before wiring them.

*Y*ou will need

2 yd. (1.85 m) each of three ribbons
  or 6 yd. (5.5 m) of one ribbon

Scissors

26-gauge craft wire

Wire cutter

One–Sided

1. Cut a 9" (23 cm) length of wire, and set it aside. From one end of the ribbon, measure the desired length of the tail. Pick up the ribbon in your left hand at this point. Gather the ribbon and pinch it tightly between the thumb and index finger, leaving the tail hanging down and the working end of the ribbon turned upward.

2. With the working end of the ribbon, form a loop of the desired size. Gather the ribbon at the base of the loop, slip it between your thumb and index finger, and hold the layers together. Now you have a downward tail and one upward loop.

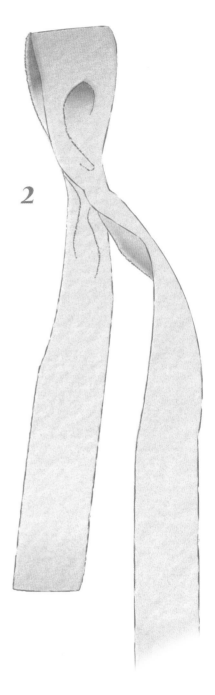

2

3

3. Turn the working end of the ribbon upward, just below your fingers. Pinch the ribbon and hold it together with the first layer.

4. Form another loop. Pinch the ribbon at the base of the loop and hold it together with the other layers.

5. Repeat steps 3 and 4 one more time, so you have three loops. Allow the working end of the ribbon to hang down. Wire the loop cluster together tightly just above the loop bases, and cut the wire ends short.

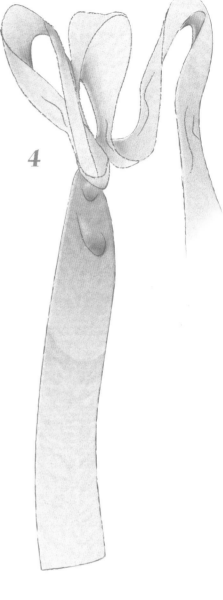

4

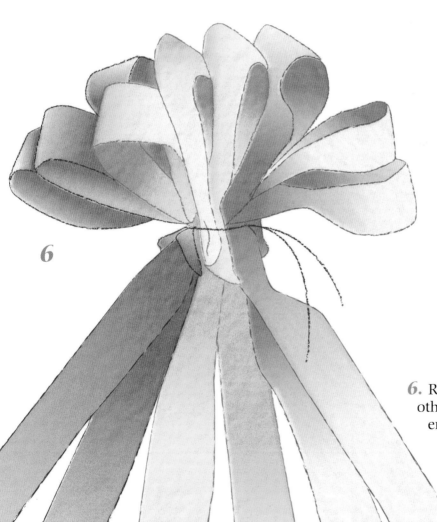

6

6. Repeat steps 1 to 5 for each of the other two ribbons, leaving the wire ends of the last loop cluster long. Use the long wires to wrap the three clusters together. Arrange the loops, intermingling the different ribbons slightly. Trim the tails at an angle.

Pompom

THIS IS THE MOST POPULAR BOW FOR GIFT PACKAGES and is very easy to make. Pompom bows can be made in nearly any size, scaled to the ribbon width and the size of the gift package. The bow shown is made from 2¼ yd. (2.1 m) of 1½" (39 mm) ribbon and is 4" (10 cm) in diameter. Plaid, patterned, solid-colored, and sheer ribbons can all be used for pompom bows.

You will need

1½ to 2½ yd. (1.4 to 2.3 m) ribbon,
  ⅝" to 2¼" (15 to 56 mm) wide

Scissors

Cardboard

26-gauge craft wire

Wire cutter

Pompom

1. Cut a 9" (23 cm) length of wire and set it aside. Cut a square of cardboard equal in width to the desired finished width of the bow.

2. Align one end of the ribbon to the bottom front of the cardboard. Wrap the ribbon around the cardboard eight to ten times, ending on the back of the cardboard.

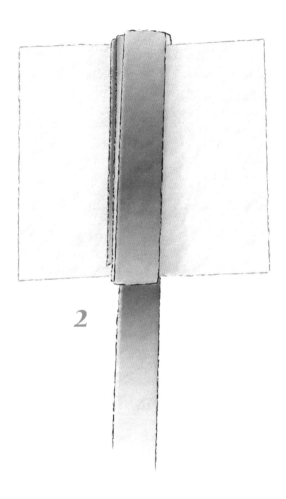

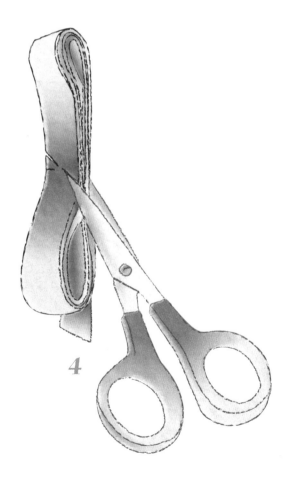

3. Carefully pull the ribbon off the cardboard. Fold the loops in half and crease the fold to mark the center.

4. Unfold the loops. On one side at the crease, cut into the ribbon edges at an angle to within ¼" (6 mm) of the center. Repeat on the opposite side.

5. Wrap the loops tightly with wire, sliding the wire into the angled cuts. Leave the wire ends long.

6. Hold the loops vertically. Slip your right index finger into the middle of the upper loops and pull out the innermost loop. Give the loop and little twist, and pull it toward the center of the bow.

6

8

7. Slip your left index finger into the middle of the upper loops and pull out the next loop. Give the loop a little twist, and pull it toward the center of the bow.

8. Continue pulling the upper loops to opposite sides and twisting them in various directions.

9. Turn the bow so the other stack of loops is on top. Repeat steps 6 to 8. Adjust the loops and fluff the bow.

10. If ribbon tails are desired, cut a length of ribbon suitable to the size of your bow, and wire it to the back of the bow. Trim the bow tails diagonally.

Starburst

*T*HE STARBURST BOW SEEMS TO RADIATE EXCITEMENT, with short V-cut tails at the top and bottom. Wired to the narrow section of an autumn wall swag, as shown, the starburst bow accentuates the rich, warm colors and offers a distinctive texture contrast to the leaves and twigs. A starburst bow adds a special touch to a gift package. Small starburst bows made from velvet ribbon make elegant napkin rings for a special occasion.

You will need

1¾ yd. (1.6 m) ribbon,
  2¼" (56 mm) wide
Scissors
26-gauge craft wire
Wire cutter
Glue

Starburst

1. Cut a 9" (23 cm) length of wire, and set it aside. Pick up the end of the ribbon in your left hand with the right side facing you. Gather the ribbon and pinch it tightly between the thumb and index finger, with the fingers pointing up, leaving the working end of the ribbon to the right.

2. With the working end of the ribbon, form a loop of the desired size. Gather the ribbon at the base of the loop, slip it under the thumb over the first layer, and hold the layers together. Now you have one loop on the right.

3. With the working end of the ribbon, form a loop of the same size on the left. Pinch the ribbon together at the base of the second loop, slip it under your thumb over the other layers and hold the layers together.

4. Repeat steps 1 and 2 to form a second set of loops, and hold them alongside the first set. Cut off the excess ribbon.

5. Wrap the bow center tightly with wire (page 7).

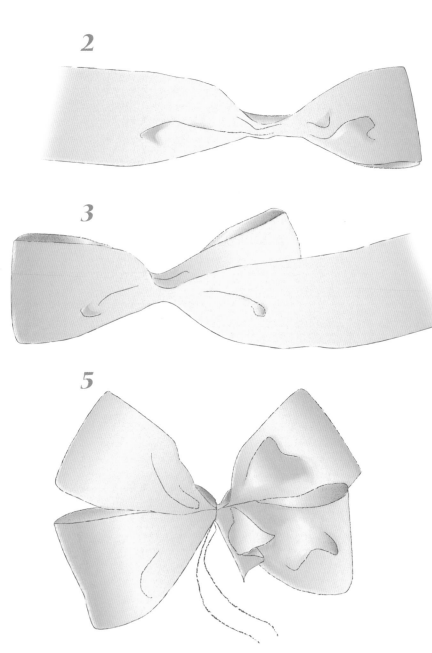

6

6. Cut two 14" (35.5 cm) lengths of ribbon. Holding the bow with the loops to the right and left, gather the 14" ribbons in the center and wire one to the top and one to the bottom of the bow. You now have two tails at the top and two tails at the bottom of the bow.

7. Cut a 5" (12.7 cm) length of ribbon. Wrap the 5" piece of ribbon around the bow center, covering the wire. Overlap the ends at the bow back. Turn under the overlapping end and glue in place.

8. Trim the bow tails in an inverted V, leaving them slightly longer than the loops.

Floral

THIS IS THE STANDARD BOW FLORISTS USE IN MOST OF THEIR ARRANGEMENTS. It can be made with as many loops as you like and using any style or size of ribbon from 1" to 4" (2.5 to 10 cm) wide. These directions are written for double-face ribbon. For single-face ribbon, give the ribbon a half twist after forming each loop, so the right side of the ribbon always faces out. To estimate the amount of ribbon needed, double the desired bow diameter, multiply it by the desired number of loops, and add the desired length for the tails.

You will need

Ribbon, amount determined by following the formula above

Scissors

26-gauge craft wire

Wire cutter

Floral

1. Cut a 9" (23 cm) length of wire, and set it aside. From one end of the ribbon, measure the desired length of the tail. Pick up the ribbon in your left hand at this point. Gather the ribbon and pinch it tightly between the thumb and index finger, leaving the tail hanging down and the working end of the ribbon turned upward.

2. With the working end of the ribbon, form a loop of the desired size. Gather the ribbon at the base of the loop, slip it between your thumb and index finger, and hold the layers together. Now you have a downward tail and one upward loop.

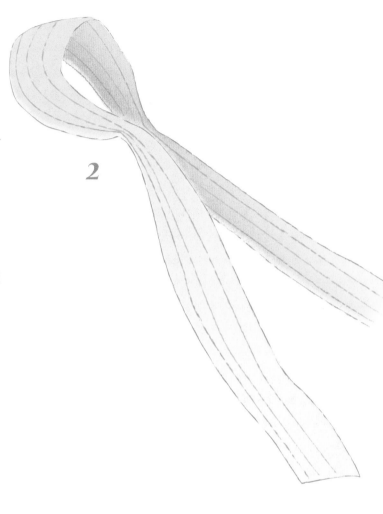

3. With the working end of the ribbon, form a loop of the same size opposite the first one. Pinch the ribbon together at the base of the second loop, slip it under your thumb over the other layers and hold the layers together.

4. Repeat steps 2 and 3 until you have the desired number of loops, evenly divided between the sides.

5. Form a small loop in the center of the bow over your thumb, and bring the ribbon under your thumb with the other layers. Insert a piece of wire through the center loop and under your thumb. Wrap the bow center with wire (page 7). Leave the wire ends long for attaching the bow.

6. Trim the second ribbon tail to the same length as the first one. Arrange and fluff the bow loops.

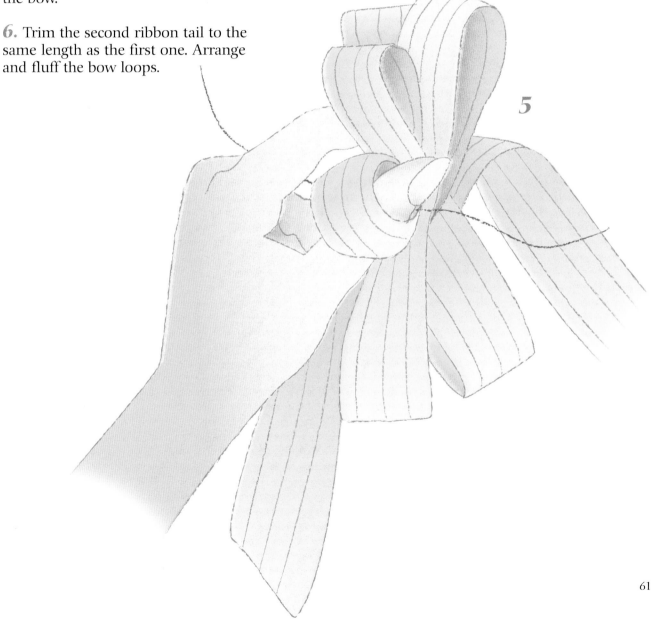

5

Asymmetrical Layers

THIS BOW HAS MORE LOOPS ON ONE SIDE than the other and several tails extending from the side with fewer loops. It is a great way to combine two or three coordinating ribbons of the same width, but can also be made with ribbons of different sizes or styles. Because of its interesting, unequal proportions, the asymmetrical layered bow is a stunning accent when placed off-center on a wreath. For an elegant look at a dinner party or reception, attach asymmetrical layered bows to the corners of chair backs. Wired-edge ribbon is recommended so the loops and tails can be easily shaped and adjusted. In these instructions, each layer is formed and wired separately and then the layers are joined together. As you become more adept at making the bow, you can form and hold all the layers at once before wiring them.

You will need

1½ yd. (1.4 m) each of three wired-edge ribbons, 1½" to 2¼" (39 to 56 mm) wide

Scissors

26-gauge craft wire

Wire cutter

Asymmetrical Layers

1. Cut a 9" (23 cm) length of wire, and set it aside. Pinch the ribbon together tightly between the thumb and index finger 10" (25.5 cm) from the end, leaving the tail hanging down and the working end of the ribbon turned upward.

2. With the working end of the ribbon, form an upward loop of the desired size. Pinch the ribbon together at the base of the loop and hold it together with the first layer. Now you have a tail and one upward loop.

3. With the working end of the ribbon, form a downward loop. Pinch the ribbon together at the base of the loop and hold it together with the other layers. Now you have a tail, one upward loop, and one downward loop.

4. Repeat steps 2 and 3 if more loops are desired. Form another upward loop. Pinch the ribbon together at the base of the loop and hold it together with the other layers. Trim off the working end of the ribbon, leaving another 10" (25.5 cm) tail.

5. Wrap the bow center tightly with wire (page 7) to complete the bottom loop cluster of the bow. Cut the wire ends short.

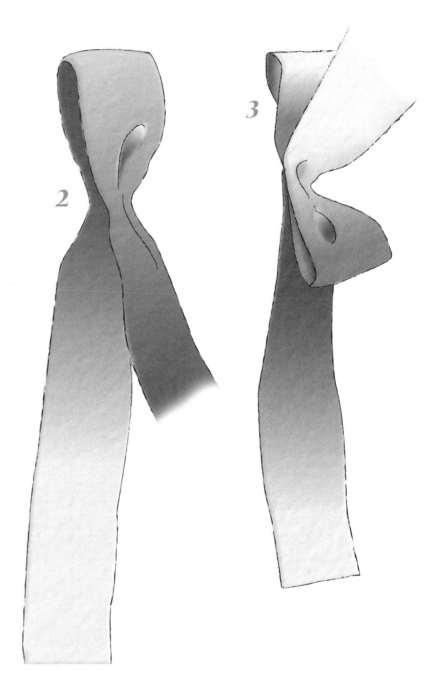

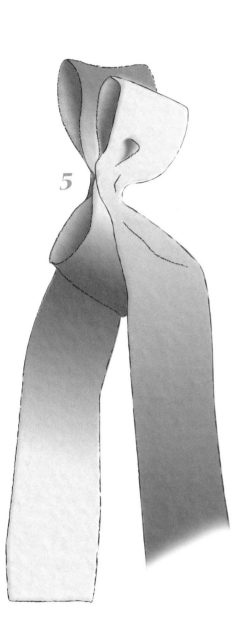

5

8

6. Repeat steps 1 to 5 with the second ribbon to make the middle loop cluster of the bow, making the tails the same length but the loops slightly smaller than the first cluster.

7. Repeat steps 1 to 5 with the third ribbon to make the top loop cluster, making the tails the same length but the loops

slightly smaller than those of the middle cluster. Do not cut the wire ends.

8. Arrange the clusters on top of each other. Secure them together with the wire ends from the top cluster. Adjust the loops and tails, hiding the wire with the smaller loops of the top layer.

Grand

THESE LARGE BOWS WITH LONG STREAMERS ARE PERFECT FOR AN ELEGANT EVENT, such as a wedding. They can be attached to chair backs, garlands, or church pews. Grand bows are made in three layers of coordinating ribbon loops. Flowing tails of various ribbon styles and widths are added to balance the top and add texture and movement. Sprigs of ivy, small silk flowers, or wired pearl picks can be glued into the bow center among the loops.

You will need

4½ yd. (4.15 m) wired-edge ribbon,
  2¼" (56 mm) wide

3 yd. (2.75 m) wired-edge sheer ribbon,
  1½" (39 mm) wide

2 yd. (1.85 m) of each ribbon desired for tails

Scissors

26-gauge craft wire

Wire cutter

Grand

1. Make a six-loop bow about 10" (25.5 cm) in diameter, with 1" (2.5 cm) tails, using the widest ribbon. (Follow steps 1 to 4 on page 27 for a four-loop bow and add another loop on each side.) Wrap the bow with wire (page 7). Cut the wire ends short, and set aside.

2. Using the same ribbon, make a four-loop bow with no center loop or tails and the same size loops as the six-loop bow. Cut the wire ends short, and set aside.

3. Using the same ribbon, make a loop the same size as the bow loops, and leave two long tails. Wire the loop at the base and set aside.

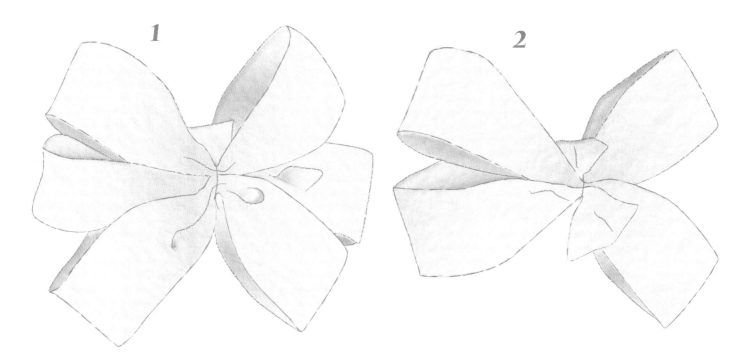

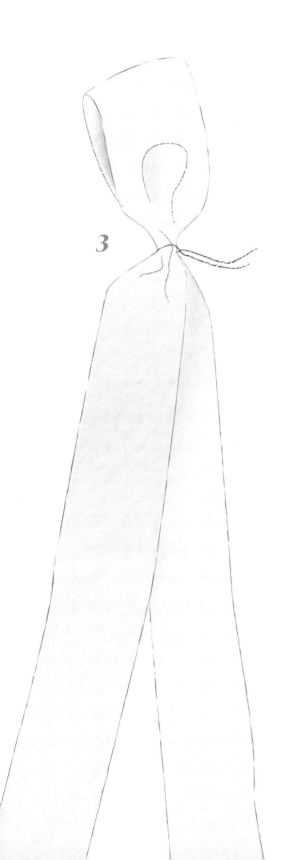

3

4

4. Make a 12-loop bow with no tails and no center loop, using the narrower sheer ribbon. Make the loops about 4" (10 cm) long. Wrap the bow with wire, leaving the wire ends long.

5. Layer the sheer bow over the four-loop bow and the six-loop bow. Wire all together, using the wire tails of the sheer bow.

6. Cut several long lengths of narrow ribbon for streamers and wire them to the back of the bow. Tie small "love knots" in the streamers at various places, if desired.

7. Wire the loop and tails from step 3 onto the back of the bow. The loop will fill the empty space at the top of the grand bow. Trim the wide tails and narrow streamers to the desired lengths.

Bow Combinations

Make a pompom bow (page 52) with two coordinating ribbons of different widths. Layer the narrow wrapped ribbon over the wide wrapped ribbon and wire the centers together before pulling the loops out into place. The narrower loops will form the center of the pompom, surrounded by the wider loops.

Make a six-loop bow of double-face satin ribbon, following the directions for a two-loop bow on page 22 and adding two more loops on each side. Glue a silk flower blossom to the center of the bow.

Layer a starburst bow (page 55) over a six-loop bow for an exciting effect that resembles a comet. Choose two satin ribbons in bright contrasting colors. Use sheer, metallic, wired-edge ribbon for the four short tails of the starburst, and leave the bright tails of both layers long.

Curled

*T*O MAKE A LARGE GIFT PACKAGE LOOK REALLY
EXTRAVAGANT, top it with a lively mound of curled ribbon.
Curling ribbon is available in 250 to 500 yd. (230 to 560 m) spools
and is relatively inexpensive, so you can keep several colors on
hand. Choose two or more colors to coordinate with the wrapping
paper. The more color the better! The curled ribbon bow looks best
when it forms a casual, tangled cluster.

*Y*ou will need

*20 yd. (18.4 m) curling ribbon, divided
   between two or more colors*

Scissors

Curled

1. Wrap one color of ribbon around the gift package. Tie a knot on the package top where you want the bow to be centered, leaving the tails about 12" (30.5 cm) long.

2. Wrap another color of ribbon around the package in the opposite direction and tie a knot over the first knot, leaving similar tails.

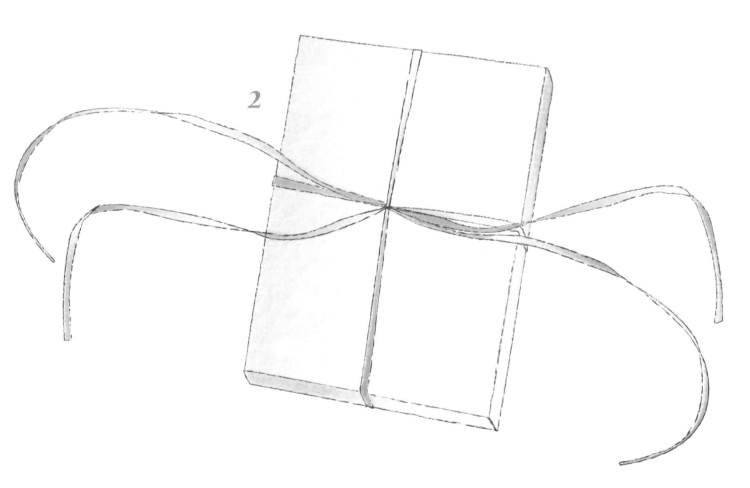

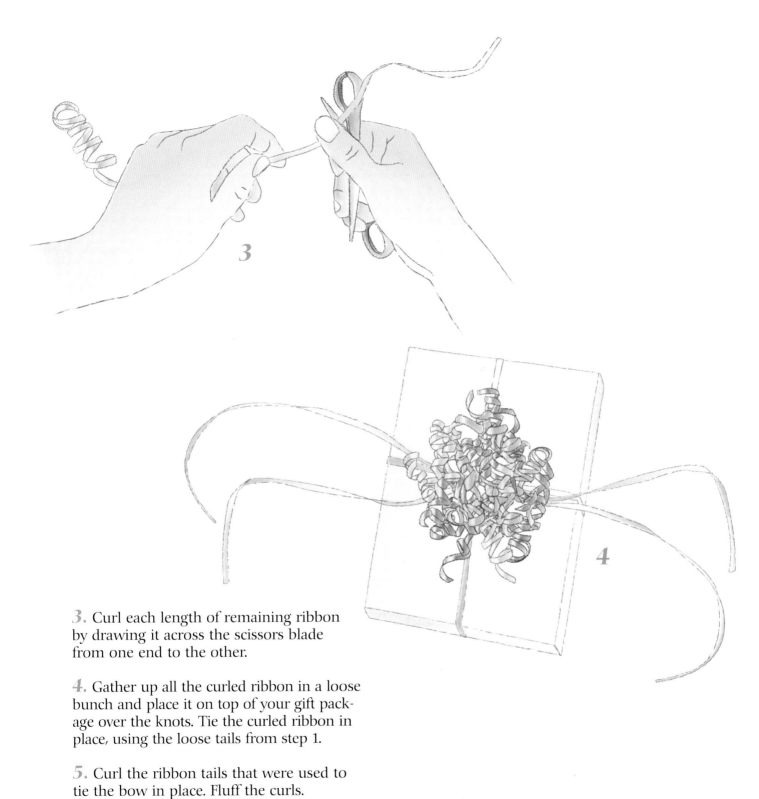

3. Curl each length of remaining ribbon by drawing it across the scissors blade from one end to the other.

4. Gather up all the curled ribbon in a loose bunch and place it on top of your gift package over the knots. Tie the curled ribbon in place, using the loose tails from step 1.

5. Curl the ribbon tails that were used to tie the bow in place. Fluff the curls.

*W*all Display

A BOW HUNG ABOVE FRAMED ARTWORK IS A HANDSOME WALL ACCENT. The color and style of the ribbon and the size of the bow should reflect the style and scale of the picture. The bow can be made with two tails that are spread slightly apart, as in the photo at left, or with one tail that hangs straight behind one picture or several small pictures. The bow is not meant to hold the weight of the picture. Rather, the bow is first hung on the wall and the picture is then mounted a short distance below the bow, over the tails. To accent an 8" × 10" (20.5 × 25.5 cm) frame, you will need about 3 yd. (2.75 m) of ribbon. Adjust the ribbon amount according to the project and number of tails.

*Y*ou will need

3 yd. (2.75 m) ribbon in desired width

Scissors

26-gauge craft wire

Wire cutter

Glue

Wall Display

1. Make a four-loop bow without a center loop or tails (page 26), making the bow in a width that suits the picture size. Wrap the center of the bow with wire (page 7), and cut the wire ends short.

2. Make a two-loop bow without tails (page 18) of the same width. Wrap the center of the bow with wire (page 7), and leave the wire ends long. Wire the small bow on top of the large bow. Leave the wire ends long, and spread them apart to the left and right.

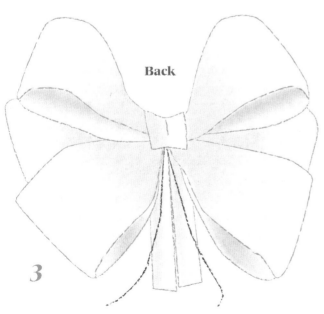

Back

3. Cut a 5" (12.7 cm) piece of ribbon. Fold the long edges to the center back. (For the bow shown on page 76, the ribbon was folded in half so the stripes would show.) Wrap the ribbon around the bow center, hiding the wire in front and allowing the wire ends to extend to the sides in back. Overlap the ends at the bow back. Turn under the overlapping end and glue in place.

Back

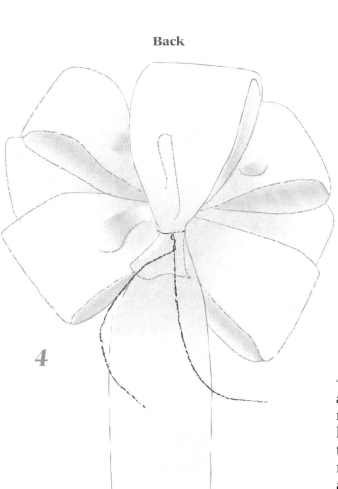

4

4. To create a bow with two tails, form a loop in the center of the remaining ribbon the same size as the other bow loops. For one tail, form a loop at the top of the remaining ribbon. Pinch the ribbon together at the base of the loop and wire it to the back of the bow.

5. Trim the bow tail(s) in an inverted V at the desired length.

*F*an

*F*OLDED RIBBON FANS CAN DECORATE GIFT PACKAGES, a Christmas tree, or a wreath. They can also be tied to dinner napkins for an elegant table accent. Choose a solid-color or printed ribbon for the fan; wired-edge ribbon holds the creases nicely. Tie the bottom of the fan with a narrow coordinating ribbon.

*Y*ou will need

*22" (56 cm) wired-edge ribbon for fan,
   4" (10 cm) wide*

*12" (30.5 cm) coordinating ribbon for tie,
   ¼" (7 mm) wide*

Scissors

26-gauge craft wire

Wire cutter

Fan

1. Cut a 9" (23 cm) length of wire, and set it aside. Place the ribbon face down, vertically on the table. Fold the bottom up ½" (1.3 cm).

2. Turn the ribbon over and fold the bottom up another ½" (1.3 cm).

3. Continue to accordion-pleat the ribbon until you have at least ten pleats, ending with the right side facing out so both cut ends are toward the back of the fan. Cut off the remaining ribbon.

3

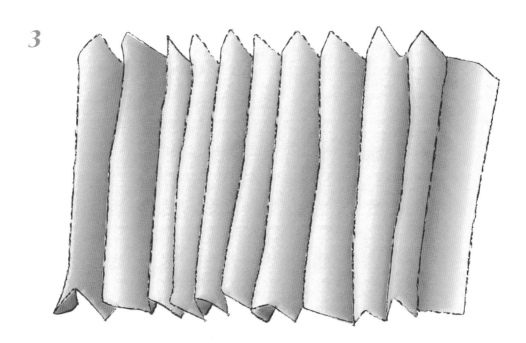

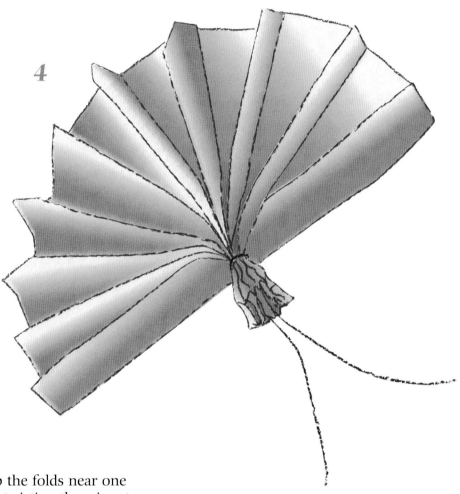

4. Tightly wrap the folds near one edge with wire, twisting the wire at the back of the fan. Leave the wire ends long if they will be needed to attach the fan to a Christmas tree branch or wreath.

5. Spread the free edge into a fan shape. Make a small shoestring bow (page 14) with narrow ribbon and glue it to the fan front over the wire.

Pinwheel

THIS CHARMING BOW CAN BE MADE WITH ONE RIBBON OR TWO DIFFERENT RIBBONS. Wired-edge ribbon works best because you can adjust the positions of the pinwheel spokes and they will stay where you want them. The wire at the center of the pinwheel bow can be hidden with small embellishments, such as pine cones or beads, or it can be covered with narrow coordinating ribbon. Use pinwheel bows to decorate gift bags or boxes, choosing an accent for the center that suits the theme of the event.

You will need

64" (163 cm) wired-edge ribbon

Scissors

26-gauge craft wire

Wire cutter

Small decoration and glue, optional

Narrow coordinating ribbon, optional

Pinwheel

1. Cut a 9" (23 cm) length of wire, and set it aside. Cut the ribbon into eight 8" (20.5 cm) pieces. Fold each piece in half to mark the center; unfold.

2. Pick up a ribbon, and gather it across the center, holding it tightly between your thumb and index finger.

3. Pick up a second ribbon, gather it across the center, and hold it together tightly alongside the first one.

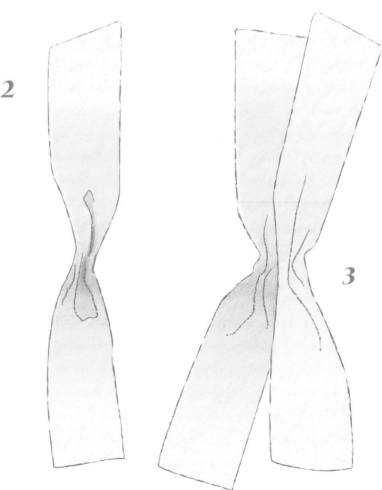

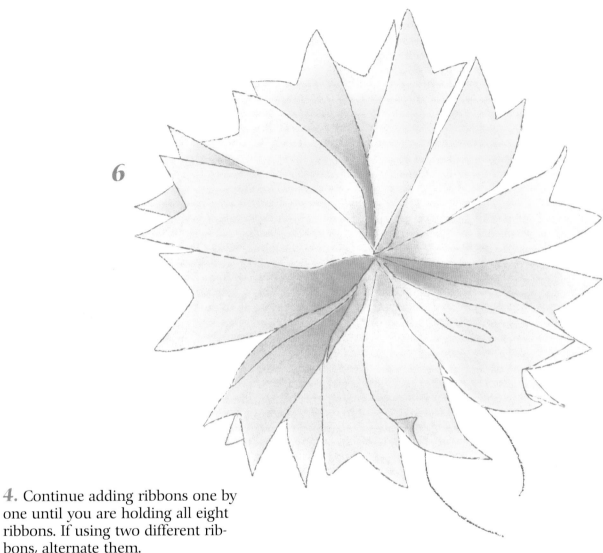

6

4. Continue adding ribbons one by one until you are holding all eight ribbons. If using two different ribbons, alternate them.

5. Tightly wrap the ribbon centers together with wire (page 7).

6. Fan out the ribbons into a pinwheel shape. Trim the ribbon ends into an inverted V.

7. Glue a small decoration to the bow center or tie narrow coordinating ribbon over the wire.

Poinsettia

*T*HE POINSETTIA IS THE TRADITIONAL CHRISTMAS FLOWER.
This ribbon poinsettia makes a beautiful Christmas package decoration. You can
also use it to accent a centerpiece or decorate your holiday tree, wreath, or swag.
Red and green satin or velvet ribbons make elegant, realistic poinsettia bows.
You can make glamorous poinsettia bows from metallic ribbons. Glue small
gold buttons or beads to the center to finish off the flower and hide the wire.

*Y*ou will need

*1½ yd. (1.4 m) red ribbon,
1½" (39 mm) wide, for the petals*

*9" (23 cm) of green or gold ribbon,
1½" (39 cm) wide, for the leaves*

Scissors

26-gauge craft wire

Wire cutter

Glue

Gold buttons or beads

Poinsettia

1. Cut two 9" (23 cm) lengths of wire, and set them aside. Cut four 8" (20.5 cm) pieces and three 6" (15 cm) pieces of red ribbon. Trim the ends into points. Fold each piece in half to mark the center; unfold.

2. Pick up a long ribbon, and gather it across the center, holding it tightly between your thumb and index finger.

3. Pick up the other long ribbons, one at a time; gather them across the center, and hold them together tightly alongside the first one.

4. Tightly wrap the ribbon centers with wire (page 7). Cut the wire ends short. Fan the petals out evenly. Set aside.

3

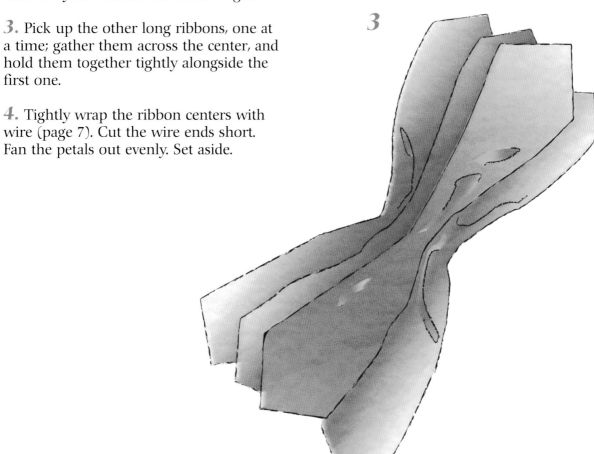

5

6

Back

5. Repeat steps 2 to 4 with the short pieces, but leave the wire ends long. Wire the short petals over the long petals, leaving the wire ends long.

6. Trim the ends of the leaf ribbon into points. Gather the ribbon across the center and wire it to the back of the poinsettia bow. Leave the wire ends long for attaching the poinsettia bow, if desired.

7. Glue gold buttons or beads to the center of the poinsettia, covering the wire.

Gathered Rose

A GATHERED RIBBON ROSE ADDS A ROMANTIC TOUCH
to gifts or fashion accessories. Attach one to a pin to make a stylish
handbag accent or lapel pin. Gathered ribbon roses can be nestled among
the leaves of a table swag or used to decorate a holiday tree. This method
for making a ribbon rose uses the wire that is woven into the edge of the
ribbon as a gathering thread to ruffle the ribbon and form the rose shape.
Craft wire, which is stronger than the ribbon wire, is used to secure the
ribbon leaves to the underside of the rose. The outer edges of the rose
"petals" can be crimped and shaped to mimic a real rose.

*Y*ou will need

1¼ yd. (1.15 m) wired-edge ribbon,
  1½" to 2¼" (39 to 56 mm) wide, for the rose

6" (15 cm) ribbon, 1½" to 2¼" (39 to 56 mm) wide,
for the leaf/tails

Scissors

26-gauge craft wire

Wire cutter

Gathered Rose

1. Tie a loose knot in the end of the long ribbon, leaving a ½" (1.3 cm) tail.

2. At the opposite end of the ribbon, pull the wire out along one edge. Gently ease the ribbon along this wire down to the knot until the ribbon is gathered to about half its original length. Do not cut the wire.

3. Holding the ½" (1.3 cm) tail, wrap the gathered edge tightly around the knot one complete round, to form the rose center.

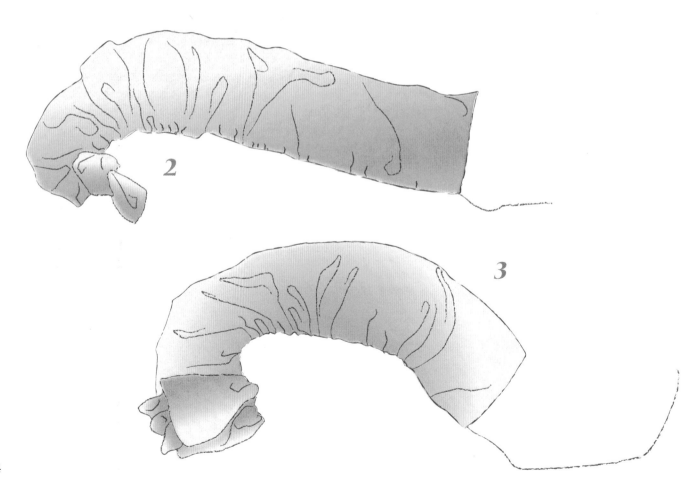

5

6

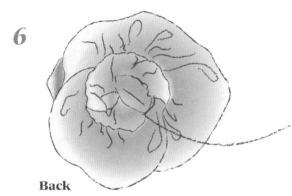

Back

7

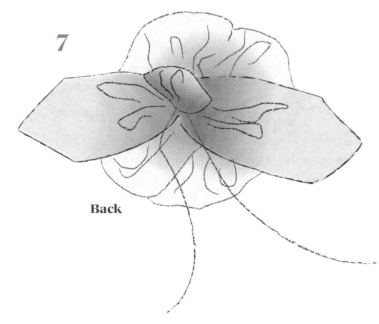

Back

4. Continue wrapping the gathered edge around the rose center, spiraling slightly further away with each wrap so the ruffled edge flares out into an open rose form.

5. Fold the ribbon under diagonally at the end so the raw edge is slightly below the gathered edge.

6. Hold the ½" (1.3 cm) tail below the knot, and secure the folded ribbon end to the rose center by wrapping the wire tightly several times around the base of the knot, catching the raw edge under the wire. Cut off excess wire.

7. Cut a 9" (23 cm) length of craft wire, and set it aside. Trim the ends of the leaf ribbon into points. Fold the center of the leaf ribbon over the short tail of the rose. Wrap tightly with craft wire at the base of the center knot. Leave the wire tails long for attaching the rose, if desired.

95

Luxury Rose

Layer a large, satin, gathered-ribbon rose over a one-sided bow for a glamorous touch on a special gift or as a luxurious fashion accent. Follow steps 1 to 6 on page 94 for the ribbon rose. Then follow the directions for the one-sided bow on page 48, substituting the ribbon rose for the top layer.